Thanks, Gary!

Leo Gohort

Textbooks?

Not yet—We Must Teach Character First!

Leah C. Tolbert

authorHOUSE®

AuthorHouse™
1663 Liberty Drive
Bloomington, IN 47403
www.authorhouse.com
Phone: 1-800-839-8640

© 2011 Leah C. Tolbert. All rights reserved.

No part of this book may be reproduced, stored in a retrieval system, or transmitted by any means without the written permission of the author.

First published by AuthorHouse 4/1/2011

ISBN: 978-1-4520-1742-6 (sc)
ISBN: 978-1-4520-1743-3 (dj)
ISBN: 978-1-4520-1744-0 (e)

Library of Congress Control Number: 2011901339

Printed in the United States of America

Any people depicted in stock imagery provided by Thinkstock are models, and such images are being used for illustrative purposes only. Certain stock imagery © Thinkstock.

This book is printed on acid-free paper.

Because of the dynamic nature of the Internet, any Web addresses or links contained in this book may have changed since publication and may no longer be valid. The views expressed in this work are solely those of the author and do not necessarily reflect the views of the publisher, and the publisher hereby disclaims any responsibility for them.

To Gregory, for being so loving to our beautiful children. And, to mother and daddy for making my life worthwhile.

Thank you.

Contents

Chapter 1: The First Day of School	1
Why the First Day Matters Most	3
Day 1	5
Table 1.1	10
Table 1.2	11
Chapter 2: The Second Day of School	13
Day Two	15
Table 2.1	18
Table 2.2	21
Chapter 3: Day Three: Textbooks Are Out for Now	23
Day Three	25
Table 3.1	30
Chapter 4: The Fourth Day of School	31
Day Four	33
Chapter 5: Ending Week One	37
Day Five	39
Table 5.1	42
Chapter 6: Building a Theme and Teaching Skills without the Textbook	43
Sentence Structure Example:	47
Homework Example:	49
Table 6.1	52
Table 6.2	53
Table 6.3	54

Chapter 7: Plan with Other Teachers as Often as You Can   57

Chapter 8: TCF for the Teacher- Make Use of Professional Development Opportunities Early and Often   63
- #1 Classroom/Behavior Management   67
- #2 Effective Use of Technology   70
- Worksheet #1   72
- Worksheet #2   73

Chapter 9: More TCF for the Teacher- Allowing Student Evaluations as another Type of Professional Development   75
- A Personal Story   78
- Worksheet #1   82
- Worksheet #2   83
- Worksheet #3   84

Chapter 10: More on Management—How to Reach the Unreachable: Dare to Think Outside the Box   85

Chapter 11: Putting It All Together   95

Resources   99

Introduction

I HAD BEEN PONDERING over writing this book for quite some time. However, each time I decided to put my thoughts down on paper, I hesitated. The topic, I knew, would be about educating children. Only, I thought, what is the big deal about that? All you have to do is get children involved in the learning process and treat them as though they matter. Then, students become so motivated you do not have to do anything but facilitate. Then it hit me—hey, just because teachers have a passion for educating, that does not mean the teacher has the tools with which to exercise that passion in an effective manner. Some people who are really interested in teaching children may not really know what works. So I began developing this work. Although the format may seem a bit informal at times, please understand the desire I have to move away from delivering a set of theories and generalizations as we often hear. Rather, I seek only to share with you what I know to be effective and practical when working with students based on what has worked for me. All children can and will learn. The key is that we must give them the tools they need with which to attain success. Without those tools, we are wasting both their time and ours, neither of which we can afford to do. I love working with children and want to see all educators be successful in their efforts to reach every student who enters their classrooms. The concepts discussed here are universal. The principles discussed are timeless. So my prayer is that you will enjoy this simple yet quite practical approach to reaching kids in any school, at any age, at any time. Thanks for your desire to educate children.

Enjoy!

Chapter 1: The First Day of School

FIRST THINGS FIRST—let us address the ever-present question asked by all. How do we get *all* our students involved in learning to the point that they are trying to be successful in any environment? Well, that is easy. We engage them from the beginning. We make them know we care about who they are, their family lives, what they like and consider important from day one. Then, we never stop. What teachers fail to realize is that we cannot engage students only in the first nine-week period of school! It has to be a continual effort throughout the entire school year.

Consistency is the key. There is no such thing as being somewhat consistent with your approach to teaching children. You either are or you are not. And guess what? Contrary to popular belief, students do know the difference no matter what grade level they are. So, for the remainder of our discussion together, we will start at the beginning. I am going to take us through some initial classroom principles that, if started on day one and used consistently, will last us the entire school year. This will be direct and to the point.

We will discuss strategies for success that will assist you in developing students who are excited about learning, but please know that they will only work if done on a consistent basis. If your plan is to engage students for the first nine weeks or only the first semester, I advise you to do one thing—close this book.

Otherwise, let us begin.

Why the First Day Matters Most

BECAUSE WE LIVE IN an often rude and immorally driven society, it is important that we begin school with the TCF approach. This stands for *teaching character first*. Please understand that by character, I do not just mean the empathy and kindness part. When we talk about character, we also mean respect and responsibility. Often, students cannot act with kindness and compassion because they do not know how to be responsible for their day-to-day actions and obligations. Nor do they know quite how that should look when engaging with others around them.

Many would suggest that we begin by handing out materials, rules, textbooks, lockers, and such. But what sense does that make if we do not first give them the tools they need in order to make informed decisions about how to use all of those materials we are so eager to send them home with each day? So many students do not get the same morals and values that were once introduced in the home just simply because of the way things are in our society. Not that it is acceptable, because I will be the first one to remind us that it is not! Yet, because TV, videos, movies, video games, and the Internet in many cases are raising our precious children, it is our job to re-instill a sense of responsibility and common decency in them when they enter our classrooms.

They have to be taught to realize that everything in life must come with a delicate balance. That which we do with a lack of moderation destroys our sense of self, and we become its slave. When we teach children to have their fun and address their academic goals in a moderate context, they learn to appreciate both. Neither of the two becomes a chore, but rather, they begin to help shape children into the productive citizens they must be in order to reach their personal and practical life successes. So let us talk about how to begin our school year.

Day 1

ON THE FIRST DAY of school, students need to be welcomed into the classroom with a smile and an open-minded attitude that nonverbally cries, "I love you, I love teaching, and I am so excited that you're here." When students enter, they need to see it on your face. They need to feel it in your handshake. They need to see it on your face throughout the entire day. If you have a bad evening just before the first day of school, that is fine. If you do not feel like being there, that is fine. Everybody has bad days with not-so-great experiences. The point is that our students often have that multiplied by a hundred.

So when students walk into our rooms, we should do whatever we have to do to make them feel as if we would not want to be anywhere else at that moment. If students feel welcomed from the first seconds they walk in the room, they are being set up for immediate acceptance of whatever we have to offer from the very first day. On the flip side, if our students think we do not want to be there and do not want them there, well, why would they want to do anything other than walk right back out the front door? So, again, let's engage them as soon as we meet them each morning.

Give a hello and flash your smile while inviting the students to take seats you have already assigned them. Though you may be tempted to allow students the freedom to sit where they please, their initial choices do need to be limited. The idea is to focus students on the structure of the classroom and your expectations on the first day. We do not want students distracted by trying to find out where their best friends from the previous year are sitting or by potential cut-up buddies for this year. By assigning seats, you have decided against fighting a battle that you would not have won anyway. Assigning initial seats also shows them that you have set controls over what goes on in terms of the structure of the room arrangement without you ever having to open your mouth and discuss the issue.

Be sure to structure the seating arrangement in a way that also engages students according to whatever assignment you have planned. If you will be mostly at the front of the room for the next few weeks, be sure to arrange clusters or rows in such a way that attention is focused on the front. If you are a teacher who will be moving around the room quite a bit, cluster the seats so that no matter where you move, no student's back is to you.

Have the first assignment on the board prior to their arrival so that students can get started as soon as they get to their seats. Have pencil, paper, note cards, or whatever other materials are necessary at the desks so there will not be any excuses about why students cannot participate in the day's first activity. Be careful not to start with a slew of negatives. "In this class, we don't do this, and you won't be doing that; this is not how we write this, and this is not how we'll draft that." Who wants to hear that? Nobody! Not them, not me, and not you. So keep things upbeat.

Once all students have arrived, begin with a short introduction of yourself, the title of your class or class theme, and what the overall requirements are. State your name as you want to be addressed. It is important to choose your title wisely based on what you want students to gain from you during the school year. Using this TCF approach teaches students to use titles that will be expected and accepted in the business world once they are out of school and at the point of entering the job market. It is important that they address you as "Mr." or "Ms." and your last name. This is what is expected of them once they enter the professional arena.

So many times, we make the mistake of letting students call us by our first names and titles, such as "Miss Amy," because we want to be seen as their friends. On the contrary, we are nurturers who are assisting the family and other support structures in guiding children through school and preparing them for the real world. Earth to all teachers: this is the real world! We teach in real classrooms, with real students, who have real issues that need to be addressed. We cannot condition them to think the real world is what hits them once they leave our classrooms. That only does the reverse and sets them up for failure once they realize the real world is where they have been all along.

After introducing yourself, the course, and your overall expectations of the curriculum, students need to engage in their first TCF lesson.

It starts with us setting the standards. It is better known as making the rules. Traditionally, we hand out a list of school rules that is at least five or so pages long, and then supply students with our two- to three-page copy of what is expected of them behaviorally in our classes. Let us abandon tradition for a moment. Just pretend for a minute that students actually have something to contribute that first day and every day (because they do), and ask what they think about what is necessary in order to foster learning in their classrooms. Yes, "their" classrooms. That is the first step in the TCF approach. We have to make students know that they not only have voices but that their voices matter. Students have to be made to feel as if their opinions count. So we show them that in order to build a classroom learning environment that hinges on mutual respect, kindness, compassion, and active learning, there has to be an understanding by all who enter the room that though there are some definite non-negotiable items, there are others we decide on as a group, which everybody will be not only asked but required to abide by in order to reach the goals this year.

In my class, I refer to the creation of rules or guidelines as the TCF code. It can also be called a class creed, conduct code, governing statement, guidelines for success, or a code of conduct. Call it what you like, but be careful not to even mention the word "rules." Students are more receptive to following rules if they are designed in such a way that is non-threatening from the beginning.

Let me explain the process of developing the class guidelines by giving an example of how I develop my plan with my students. I begin with the basic concepts of success and respect. I tell students as a whole group that in order for everyone to be successful this school year, every one of us must foster an environment that is respectful of ourselves as well as of others. Students must be made to realize immediately that their actions and reactions in class affect the learning or lack thereof of other students and vice versa. So, we start by putting a blank page up on the projector.

For the morning work, students have already been guided to write their definitions of what respect looks like or means to them on note cards that have been provided at their desks. I give students a chance to volunteer (not necessarily raising hands—we will address that later on) to read their ideas about respect aloud to the class. I make a line down the center of my page to divide "I see" and "I hear." At the top center, I write the word "respect" in all capital letters. We then create a dialogue of what respect looks like, sounds like, or makes them feel like. An example is shown in table 1.1.

You can set up your chart any way you like as long as it allows students to expound on their ideas about respect.
We spend the entire class period talking about and listing to as many ideas as they want. Throughout the discussion, I strategically add my own. This way, I get to insert important "rules" they may leave out, but students also see from the first few minutes on that they matter and that their ideas are valued.

The next step in developing the TCF classroom guidelines is to narrow the list. We begin to cross out ideas that are very similar or exactly stated in order for students to be able to have fewer ideas to commit to memory. Once we have a finalized list that we all feel we can live with, we leave it up for a few minutes. I ask the students to then share with a neighbor or write privately at their desks one thing they know and like about the TCF classroom code. The entire time, I am moving casually around the room, encouraging productive discussion, and ensuring that students are on task discussing only what I have asked. Note that this is done casually at first. There will be a time later where I may have to become more direct or firm in my approach. However, this initial meeting is one that fosters an engagement of the students in gaining a knowledge of what I expect in class overall. The further the week progresses, the more specific, direct, and firm I become. By giving students a chance to discuss what they have learned about the TCF code, they are able to continue to process what they may otherwise have lost if they were not given that chance for discussion.

Now, we are ready to incorporate the school-wide procedural approach into our TCF class code. If students have already mentioned ideas that permeate the school, I do not bother repeating that it is a school rule per se. But if they have neglected to mention important pieces of the school plan within our class code, I incorporate those ideas, briefly emphasizing their importance. You will find an example of a finalized TCF class code in table 1.2.

I end the first day of the school year by reviewing what we have done that day. I remind students that they entered the room prepared, orderly, began their first assignments immediately, built the TCF code centered around respecting oneself and others, discussed what they learned, and are now ready for a successful school year. I let them know firmly that I expect the same grand performance from them tomorrow. I end by thanking students for their time, attendance, and participation. I let them know that I am sure they could have chosen to be somewhere else but that I am happy they chose to share their day with me. I mean, let's face it. Our students are often spending much of their days raising themselves or other siblings, or assisting at home in other ways that make them unable to function as true children but rather almost as adults in training. So it is no wonder that many of them have a number of other important things on their minds besides school.

My job is to make students feel so valued when they enter the learning environment that they will not want to think about other things that press their minds and agendas besides school. This way, for the time I am teaching, I know that I am making a lasting impression on these students that will be there when all else fails. If I want to give children the tools they need to be successful, I have to start on day one. Otherwise, anything else I do the rest of the year is done in vain. Remember, today's strategies sound good, and they will work, but you must be consistent in your approach. Thus, day two begins in much the same way.

Table 1.1

(Insert any character word in the chart as it applies to your teaching and fill spaces accordingly.)

What respectful people do (actions)	What respectful people say (sounds)
Sharing	Kind things to others
Soft voices	Please
Positive facials	"I'm sorry" when needed
Stay in their own personal space	I'll help you.
Hands to themselves	Ask before taking
Responsible for their work	Thank you
Clean up their area	May I ...

Table 1.2

(Note that you can call this any title you deem appropriate: rules, guidelines, contract, etc.)

Finalized Classroom Code of TCF

- We will respect one another in all that we say and do.
- We will work together to show kindness to each other.
- We will take care of our personal academic and behavioral responsibilities.
- We will keep ourselves in our own personal spaces.

---

*Remember to modify the language according to the age group you are teaching. Also, be sure that your code reflects the school-wide initiatives.

Chapter 2: The Second Day of School

Day Two

BE SURE STUDENTS SIT where they did yesterday by putting up a chart with their names coded according to table 2.1. Or, for younger children, you can leave the cards from yesterday on the desks with names listed there.

The first morning's assignment should already be listed on the board for students to complete. It should have to do with preparing for the class and reviewing yesterday's TCF class code and any other important issues that were introduced yesterday. Research shows that no matter what the skill, students should participate in what is called a spiral review several times a week in order to truly grasp what is being introduced. This is the only way children will transfer information into their long-term memories. When students strategically review skills, they retain them more readily and do not have to participate in rote memorization that then becomes meaningless.

Since we began by designing a TCF class code, we want to make this the first thing we review on the second day. For the morning work, students list one element from the TCF code that they remember and explain what it means to them. Then, once class begins, turn on your projector and go over the TCF code immediately. If you have a technologically savvy classroom, this would be even more engaging for the students if done through PowerPoint or with an Elmo. By creating a list and then seeing the previous day's list, students are able to automatically review twice what is expected of them for the day. There are no excuses! Now that everyone knows what is expected, the day's lesson will flow more easily than if the children were unsure.

Once the tone has been set for what is expected school wide as well as within the classroom, it is time to familiarize students with how and why your classroom is set up the way it is. I will walk us through this process by discussing how I take students on a tour through my room.

I start by noting the way I want students to enter the classroom. I model for them both the improper way (running, pushing, jumping, etc.) as well as the proper way (walking, reviewing board work, heading directly to their seats). We can never assume that students already know anything even if they are seniors in high school. We must teach everything we want them to truly understand. This is directly in contrast to what we often do. Usually, the older students are, the less modeling we do for them. But think about it. Prior to the first day of school, when have students ever entered *your* classroom? NEVER! So for them to enter based on their previous experiences is perfectly logical. If students have been entering classrooms inappropriately five or six years before entering yours, or acting however they want in their at-home settings, what makes you think that just because you expect different that they will actually get it right?

So we must model both ways if we expect for students to not only take us seriously but also to perform in the expected way on a daily basis.

The next important thing I go over is how I want students to head their papers. For the entire year (remember, consistency), I head my front board the same way they should head their papers so that there is no need for questioning it on a regular basis. Of course, this can be done team wide by each grade level, which is more effective as students do not have to keep relearning a heading. Or if you are in a self-contained teaching environment, it can be whatever works for the subjects you are teaching.

Then, I note the left corner of the front board and how it is reserved for preparatory work. Here, I list that pencils should be sharpened and that paper and books should be out, and any other important last-minute reminders for the time period are given. I also list here the first assignment that reviews the previous day's major skill. An example is provided in table 2.2.

After familiarizing students with the front board, I talk them through the classroom bulletin boards, letting the children know the theme of each one. One is devoted to the calendar, one for skills, and one for famous quotes that relate to the subjects I am teaching that year, and the final board is for students to fill with their work. I then explain to students about other posters, quotations, and items that are displayed throughout the room. I note which areas are designated for their enjoyment and which areas are off limits, like my teacher desk work space.

You may be wondering why this is deemed as important for the second day of school. It goes back to the TCF approach to learning. We have to teach students the skills we want them to embrace. By noting the enjoyment versus the off-limit areas for our students, we are setting them up for immediate success every time they enter the room. Again, we must assume *nothing* in regard to what we would like for the children to know. If I never tell a student not to sit at or pick things up from my desk, I do not have a right to be upset with him if he does either of the two. I cannot discipline for something I have not taught. So remember, just as we teach academics, we must use the TCF approach to learning and teach the behaviors we want to see as well.

Table 2.1

Seating Chart ideas

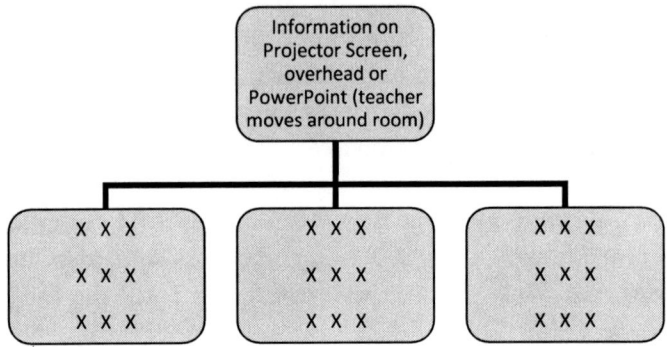

*Having desks in rows is really only good for these types of presentations where students can be fully focused on the information being presented directly from the front of the room.

*This *should not* be used on a regular basis.

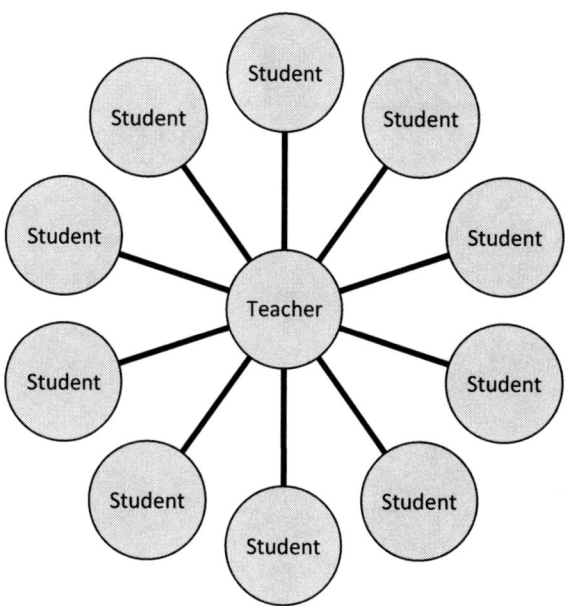

*This seating chart is good for rap sessions, whole group discussions, and whole group presentations where students get more of a community feel and can engage with one another.

*You can also use this design to have students turn to their left or right for mini discussions regarding a topic you have given them.

(continue to next page)

> Teacher moves around the room as a facilitator.

X X   X X
X X   X X

X X   X X
X X   X X

X X   X X
X X   X X

*Depending on how many students you have, this is an ideal seating arrangement. Students are paired in threes or fours in order to interact effectively in discussions, projects, and activities. They are able to become effective self-managers, and character development is a given.

*This is the seating arrangement I use most often.

Table 2.2

This is daily information to have on the board *before* the children arrive. You can have however much you want on the board, but remember, it is a session starter for them. It need not be that extensive. Consistency is the key.

Name
Date
Subject

Tasks:
1. Turn in homework.
2. Sharpen pencils.
3. Take out journals.
4. Head papers.
5. Complete morning work.

Morning work: Answer questions below.
1. $34 - 18 =$
2. $54 \times 10 =$
3. Bryan and ___ walked home. (me, I)
4. The soup ___ boiling. (is, are)

Chapter 3: Day Three: Textbooks Are Out for Now

Day Three

PLEASE REMAIN MINDFUL OF the fact that I am speaking from my personal experiences and what I *know* works in the classroom. I have taught grades two through eight at some point in my career with an emphasis in language arts at each level. I also teach reading and writing in a local GED program. This includes writing, using basic grammar and speaking skills, reading, and creative thinking skills. At some points, I have also taught in self-contained classrooms where the focus has been all subjects. Though I currently teach elementary school, most of my experience has been at the middle school level with fifth through eighth grades and with high school age students up through age fifteen. So, for the remainder of the book, I will be speaking primarily from a middle school reference point, remembering that these principles do work for all children. With that said, I also want you to remember that setting the standard regarding your classroom expectations remains vital at all grade levels. It is not just a middle school need.

Surely we all know this, but by now, you are probably in panic mode, wondering when we are going to discuss academics. After all, this is an academic setting—the classroom, right? Right. But you have to remember that our approach is slightly different. TCF, *teaching character first*, is the key to getting the academics to flow properly once we are ready to introduce our lessons. So this third day of school will continue to focus mostly on character development with a bit of the academics in the mix.

Developmentally, the middle-aged student is torn between two zones. He or she is not sure whether to consider him or herself a child or a teenager. These students are dissatisfied with referencing themselves as "preteens." So school becomes progressively difficult for them at this point. I have often taught students who were fifteen or sixteen in the eighth grade because of various situations that have caused them to fall behind in school. It is even more difficult for this type of student to feel as though he or she belongs and can be successful in school. If they are not given some basic moral principles to guide their thinking back toward the direction of success, they will shut down, and you can hang up any type of academic progress, including staying in school once they enter high school. So there remains the need to continue the process of building relationships with students within the first full week of school.

Today, we take the principles we have taught and make them applicable to students' everyday experiences. I call this the TCF role-play session. You can design the role-play activities in whichever fashion fits your teaching style, but remember that students all learn according to many different learning styles. I begin the same way I do each day by directing attention to the front board. I remind students to read the preparatory work very carefully so that they will have a general idea of what the day's lesson will review and what new skills will be introduced.

For the first activity, students will not need paper and pencils but will need to pick up index cards with pre-written responses on them from me. So, as each student reads the front board, he or she will begin to come to me, pick up the index cards, and be seated.

On the index cards, I have statements listed that the students will say in response to something I say based on the TCF class code and the school-wide guidelines we have covered over the past two days. Let us discuss one example as well as how to reach the student who is not yet comfortable with responding aloud in class in a role-play situation. More situations are listed in table 3.1.

This example deals with confronting someone who is writing with your pencil you have dropped upon entering the classroom. The role-play may be carried out in the following manner:

I would read my index card, which says, "Hey! That's my pencil, girl. I don't know who you think you are, stealing my stuff."

One student who has an appropriate non-confrontational approach on his or her card may raise his or her hand to respond to me.

For example, "I'm sorry. I didn't realize this was your pencil. Here you are. I found it on the floor. Next time, I'll give something I find to the teacher or ask my classmates out loud whether it belongs to someone or not before using it."

I would then read an appropriate response on my card, which says, "Oh, my bad. Thanks. Sorry, I got in your face."

At this point, we would discuss together what was wrong about the initial student's boisterous request and then note how the other person's response helped to calm down the other student rather than further agitate him or her. Now, remember that in the middle school setting, class periods only last forty-five to fifty-five minutes. So, depending on the time frame, we could reenact this same scene again to give the boisterous response and see how that type of situation would end up, or we could move on to another scenario.

Students really enjoy the role-plays. It gives them a chance to share with each other as well as with me the reasons why students often react inappropriately in various situations. It never fails that students point out in the negatively driven scenarios the fact that the one person was not showing the other one *respect*. This concept seems to be a fundamental piece of the puzzle in understanding students no matter what the grade level. Every child wants to be respected. In the world of adolescence, every response students have is based on their views of *respect*: what it is, what it is not, why they give it, and why they do not. This fits perfectly into the TCF model.

So we end day three with providing the first homework assignment of the year. For all of you who were in panic mode about academics, have no fear! Academics are here! I end day three by keying in on TCF and the concepts that drive our need for *respect*. I tell them to look at the sideboard where the evening's lesson is listed. Now, those who have already read the preparatory work carefully have already copied down the homework. If they did not, they will be rushing to write and listen to the assignment. This becomes the first lesson in reading *all* the directions carefully the first time and following them accordingly.

For the homework, students will write two paragraphs. The first one will focus on their definition of what respect looks like or means to them. The second one will focus on what being disrespectful looks like or means to them.

This assignment does several things.

For students, it does the following:

- Keeps what we have covered for the day fresh on their minds.
- Makes sure they know that their ideas count and will be shared in class in some format.
- Gives them writing practice based on skills they gained the previous year, which I can use later as a gauge for building grammar lessons.
- Makes them accountable by giving the children responsibilities that include bringing materials to class.

For teachers, it does the following:

- Provides a springboard for the next day's lesson.
- Gives you a chance to see which students are motivated to do homework and which are not.
- Gives you a quick sampling of writing skills, listening skills, cursive practice, sentence structure, general comprehension, etc.
- Can red flag students who may have further trouble in the traditional classroom setting.
- Provides you an opportunity to record a 100 percent as an "easy" grade for students who complete the assignment in order to help them feel that overall success is attainable in your classroom.

Again, this type of homework assignment is reinforcing the fact that there is not only a specific way to enter the classroom, but there is also no time to waste once we get started. From the beginning of class to the end, the students know that what they do matters! We have to get in, get started, and accomplish our goals for the day if we want to reach success. That has to be the theme of the classroom from the very beginning.

One of the worst things a child can say to me, which has become a pet peeve of mine, is "Mrs. Tolbert, are we doing anything today? And, are you taking a grade?" I tell them very firmly each time, "Yes, of course we are doing something today! We do something important every day! And, yes, I am taking a grade!"

Now, between you and me, I might take a letter grade, or I may just be evaluating participation. But I do not tell my students that. I want them to feel that everything they do is of value to me because it is. The reason I do not tell them what type of grade I am recording is because some would take "no letter grade" to mean that I am less than interested. The truth is there are many types of student assessments. There will be time to take specific grades according to the mastery of specific skills, but at this point in the TCF model, the key is to set the students up for success. The more assessment tools you use, the more students will learn to value their own efforts. Not to worry, we will come back to that later. On to day four …

Table 3.1

> **Role-Play Examples: "Act It Out"**
>
> You left your pencil at your desk, and now it is gone. What do you do?
>
> Someone pushes you (by accident or maybe on purpose) as you stand in line for lunch. Respond.
>
> Mr. X asks you again to turn around and be quiet while he is giving instructions. How do you respond?
>
> There is a rumor that you will be beaten up on your way to the bus today. Respond.
>
> Your best friend keeps cheating from your test papers. What do you do?
>
> The new girl sits in your seat in class. You are already having a bad day. What is the proper response?
>
> Mrs. Y never listens. She just yells at anyone who asks a question. How does this make you feel? What do you do about it?

*Remember, you can allow students to act out the entire scenario depending on what time permits. They can respond with the proper reaction as well as the improper reaction.

*Students often remember information that is modeled for them. We cannot expect them to act appropriately if it is not modeled for them first.

Chapter 4: The Fourth Day of School

Day Four

I WANT YOU TO CLOSE the book for a moment and try to remember the layout for what will happen at the beginning of class on today. This will be from the minute students enter the room until you as the teacher are done monitoring and ready to begin the actual lesson. When you open the book, the printed list below will help you. See how many of these you get. Ready? Go!

- Students enter the room in the appropriate manner that has already been discussed so they do not have to guess.
- Students read the preparatory work to know what is expected of them.
- If the preparatory work includes copying homework down, they do that.
- If the preparatory work includes picking up certain materials or preparing their papers, they do that.
- Then, students complete the actual assignment that is listed on the board under preparatory work.
- They sit quietly or as otherwise instructed until the actual day's lesson begins.

Okay! How many did you get? All of them in some fashion, I trust. Even if they were not worded like mine, or if you enumerated them further, I hope you are beginning to grasp the basic concept. If we spell out clearly what is expected of them, our students will perform up to par every time!

Day four's preparatory work will indicate that students should have their homework out on their desks, ready to be reviewed and recorded for a grade. Students are instructed under preparatory work also to write me a note on a sheet of notebook paper if they did not complete the assignment. There are a couple of reasons why we set up the approach to turning in the first homework assignment in this manner.

First, we have not had enough time to evaluate how trustworthy each student is yet. So we do not want them to feel judged. And second, we do not know anything about the students' backgrounds yet. There are so many variables that help determine why a student does or does not turn in homework that if we embarrass them on the front end, we may not ever get a chance to reach those who may have problems getting the work done.

The key to reaching students on day four is making them feel accepted in whatever way that takes its form. There will be time at the end of class to address students privately who did not do the homework assignment. We can give them a gentle reminder for tomorrow, stress how practice makes learning easier, and students will inevitably respond more positively than they would if we addressed them in front of their peers within this first week.

Now that we have asked students to have their homework out or write a private note saying why homework was not completed, we are ready to delve into our lesson for the day. The topic is responsibility coupled with what we already know about respect. This is such a great way to develop an appreciation for one another, the school climate and culture, as well as the surrounding school community.

Everyone wants to be respected and carry out his or her individual responsibilities as a student. Yet so often, we just say that the rule or regulation is to "show respect." Or "be responsible." Only what does that mean? I guarantee that if you ask one hundred different people on any given day of the week, you would get as many different responses as the people you ask. Why? Because of one thing—our reference points are different. All people have an idea of what respect looks like to them. So, by building day four around a discussion of what responsibility and respect are going to mean in our class, we set the students up for social successes in that we get everyone on the same page in order to reach our goal of developing respectful and responsible young citizens.

An example of one respect and responsibility activity is shown below:

1. Have students' desks arranged in groups of three or four, depending on class size.
2. Students will be asked to share one or two of the most important ideas they wrote during homework or preparatory work about respect with the rest of the group.
3. When you call on a student, he or she will share one key component of respect for you to write on the board or projection screen.
4. As students talk, write their responses for everyone to view, even if some are repeated.
5. Add your own ideas based on the school and or district guidelines that you feel need to be shared if students have not shared the same ideas.
6. Go through together and cross out any ideas that are the same or very similar; reword those that can be said in a shortened fashion.
7. Finally, you have a class view of what respect is according to all students who enter this room. Hopefully, if you are working with a teaching team, other teachers are doing similar activities to arrive at some semblance of what respect is for your grade and, ideally, for your school.
8. Repeat this activity in reference to defining responsibility. You can take this type of activity as far into discussing character traits as your schedule will allow (kindness, compassion, empathy, self-control, self-esteem, and so on).

Even if a few students are uncomfortable speaking aloud, by giving them the opportunity to avoid embarrassment if the assignment was not complete, and by allowing all students the opportunity to have their ideas expressed, we have set the classroom climate for the year. Students may not openly say it, but I guarantee you they appreciate being treated with respect and worth!

Your students will begin to show you in the way they enter the room, the way they address you and other adults in the building, and the way they treat one another. I am not suggesting that you are building a social or academic utopia, but by building a positive climate, you are setting students up for small successes that will lead to greater ones as the school year and as their academic experiences progress.

So let us finish out this first week!

Chapter 5: Ending Week One

Day Five

DEPENDING ON YOUR SUBJECT area, school rules and forms that need to be returned, etc., up until this point, you have stressed the classroom make up, entering and exiting appropriately, preparatory work, homework assignments, and all other key areas students will need to build on daily in order to be successful this school year.

Today, we need to show students we are holding up our end of the bargain, per se. Students have tried to come in appropriately, be prepared, and have listened to what we asked of them. So it is important to show our students that their work pays off immediately. Research shows that children of all ages, especially through eighth grade, need immediate feedback as well as long-term feedback in order to continue performing up to whatever standards we have set.

Now, the way you set up your grading procedures will probably be based on state or district level standards. But, very rarely does any school system tell teachers how often to grade, what types of grades to take, or when to begin. Basically, all school districts give us a minimum number of grades to be recorded and ask that we vary the assessment procedures. For this first week, it is important that students see they have achieved success. They need to know not only it is possible, but they can also do it with average to above average grades.

So, after you have introduced the preparatory work for today, you should have a PowerPoint or other type of visual prepared for the students to see how your grade book is set up for the year. Students need to see a sample name, a sample of what types of grades you will take for that grading period, and exactly what you have recorded for that week's grade.

The sample in figure 5.1 shows the students' names, the grades we have recorded for the week, and this week's class average. A simple way to do it for the first grading period is to have a grade category for attendance/participation, homework (effort-only since circumstances around completion of homework may vary), tests/quizzes, and class assignments/activities.

By giving students feedback in the first week, you have given them a reason to want to come back for the rest of that grading period. I have always hated being in a teacher's class who says they grade only on the curve system. You know, the ones who threaten you on day one by saying that As are not for everyone. Teachers, parents, and students, wake up! As, just like Fs, can be for every child.

If you give an A effort, in many cases, it should be easy for you to attain such. Of course, we are all aware that the final grade in every class for every student will not be an A, as all children are different and learn at varying levels. However, there is no reason for someone to travel thirteen years through school and never see an A or whatever grade means a high level of success for him or her. When students see that in the first week they received a high percentage in some if not all areas, they want to return. How do you make that happen? I'm glad you asked.

In this first week, grade students primarily on participation. Let the children know exactly how they have received their grades. Give them the benefit of the doubt! If they come every day, believe me, for some of them that is an effort in and of itself! Let students see their name in the grade book with a 100 percent beside it. If for some reason you must deduct points, do not go below 90 percent. Basically, you are letting the children know that you value them. Tell them verbally after showing each child his or her grades.

Finally, remember to assign homework. Yes, I know it has been a long week. However, this is for the sake of reminders. The homework for the end of this first week in the school year should be to have a healthy and safe weekend and be ready to do exciting things on Monday. Remind students that they do not want to miss what you have in store for them next week.

Give yourselves a hand! You have made it through a successful first week of school. This will get you started on a positive note. As you begin your academic lessons in the second week, the behavior and morale problems your neighbors will be having (all year) will not be of any concern to you because you have done what it takes from day one to establish a positive climate and a tone of success in your classroom. You may be a few days behind in your lesson plans, but it will pay off in the end. In the spring when everyone else is struggling to get all the skills barely covered, you will be weeks ahead of them because you started with the TCF approach.

Next, let us look at what we will be doing the rest of this first grading period.

Table 5.1

Grade Book Sample
    Assignments

Names	TCF activity	Role-play	Assignment 1	Quiz 1
Sam	100	100	88	96
Jean	100	100	83	75
Kimberly	100	100	78	99
Maria	100	100	95	81

*We understand all students learn differently and progress at varying levels. Therefore, it is crucial that we begin with a couple of activities/assignments each grading period that give them the confidence boost they need to propel themselves forward.

Chapter 6: Building a Theme and Teaching Skills without the Textbook

YOU MAY BE WONDERING why it took us so long to get through just the first five days of school. However, you will appreciate, as will your students, the time it takes to really think through how to help students be successful from day one. Remember the main key to making the TCF approach work is consistency. It does not matter if your intentions are golden. If you do not continue down the same path during the remainder of the school year, you have wasted your time and theirs, too.

So, now that we have the children's attention, we need to be sure to build the rest of this first grading period in a fashion that remains beneficial. Some of you may be in school systems where the entire curriculum is set, while others may have a skeletal framework from which to build according to the listed skills. Whichever category you fall into, be sure to structure a thematic unit that reaches your students. Because I teach language arts, I will draw from that venue.

When exploring any subject, students will ask you what they are going to learn, what the point of the lesson is, etc. Contrary to how they make us feel at times, students just want to know that what they are learning is really going to matter years from now or even later that week.

I generally teach in inner-city schools, and many times, I see students who are raising themselves and up to seven or eight other siblings in assistance to their parents. Sometimes, they do not even live with their parents. I say that to say that my students' issues when they leave school are so much more than what I could ever fathom. So, if I want them to come back the next day ready for what I have to give them, ready to take time out of their legitimately hectic schedules, I have to make what I am saying matter.

Therefore, for the remainder of this first grading period, I develop a theme that centers on character development, since that is what we started with in week one. It fits perfectly because I have already introduced the TCF code to them, we have built a framework for what respect in our classroom and school is to us, and we are getting to know one another in a manner that shows that model of respect not only in my classroom but throughout the building. I have been in conference with parents either by email, in person, or over the phone when possible, and I have met with my teammates on a regular basis before school began and throughout the first week. So everyone involved with my students knows that whatever the skill is that we are covering, we are going to tie it back to character development.

So for me to build the remainder of what we do around the theme of developing character means that students will be able to string together each mini-concept we discuss weekly into an overall concept of developing who they are from within by the end of the year. In figure 6.1, you will see a sample of how to use character development as a theme based on some of the academic areas you may teach.

You may ask how we do this and still teach the activities and skills from the textbooks. Remember the title of the book? Okay. We throw the textbooks out in a way for right now so that when we are ready to use them for needed lessons, they actually matter to the students.

For example, if I am teaching sentence structure as many language teachers do in the first few weeks of school, I could say, "Okay, students, open to page thirty-two. We are going to do exercise one, one through ten. Then, for homework, do exercise two, one through twenty." I am sure the writers of the textbooks would be so pleased to see that their efforts have not been in vain. However, what do the kids think? *Boring!* That is what they think. So I need to introduce sentence writing in a more interesting way.

Sentence Structure Example:

I MAY READ THEM a picture book like Numeroff's *If You Give a Pig a Pancake*. This is a fabulous book for introducing nouns and verbs no matter what age group you are working with in class. Students, even in middle school (and sometimes especially at that age), enjoy hearing the story, searching the pictures, and noting the nouns and verbs they have seen and heard in the story when you are ready for discussion. Once you have finished reading, do a web similar to figure 6.2, which lists their ideas. Then, you are ready to create sentences based on the nouns and verbs you have listed together. The examples can even be nonsense sentences like the fictional story as long as the rules for subject and predicate development are followed. Whatever reading selection you choose for this type of grammar lesson, the students are turned on to the learning process because the story has genuinely engaged them.

We have thrown the textbooks out, if you will, long enough to engage students and ourselves in the same type of skills practice they would have found on "page thirty-one, one through ten". Yet, our approach has been much more interesting. For homework, you can have them look around their homes for nouns and verbs in order to create three to five good sentences. This prepares us for a discussion of punctuation and capitalization the following week.

How do teachers keep the focus on character while doing these activities that do not seem to necessarily connect with character development? We do this through grouping. As students become more comfortable with working on their own, you can begin to group them according to varied learning styles, random selection, comprehension levels, student choice, etc. This would be a great time to put up the TCF code and ideas from the respect chart for review. Remind students of how they want to be treated when working with others. Let them know you expect the same of them. Remember, if you are doing this on a consistent basis as a self-contained teacher or as a team of teachers who address specific subjects, students will gradually begin to display those desired characteristics they discussed in those first five days on a regular basis.

By the end of the first nine weeks, students should be writing sentences, paragraphs, essays, or stories based on other picture books dealing with topics like attitude and behavior, respect, responsibility, and so forth. In table 6.3, you will find a list of some excellent books that are great for read-aloud lessons, discussion, and written reflection. No matter what subject area you teach, you can build in discussions about character in strategic ways that get the students interested in what you are saying and excited about learning. It does take quite a bit of planning on the front end, but you will see the fruits of your labor in the faces of children who are engaged in active learning.

Homework Example:

EVEN HOMEWORK ASSIGNMENTS SHOULD connect to what is being introduced in class. You can use the nouns and verbs "around the house" activity. Also, ask students to suggest homework assignments they think will be useful for learning whatever concept you are discussing. If you are teaching a novel, this is ideal for working with vocabulary. Why pull vocabulary from a textbook when you can pull directly from the novel you are teaching? It makes no sense. Students will remember what the story is about and be able to relate it to their own lives if they understand the vocabulary being used in the novel itself. They can do vocabulary drills at home based on the novel's vocabulary rather than from a text that does not connect to what is being learned in class.

One such novel you can adapt to your subject area is that of *The Giver* by Lois Lowry. I use this example simply because it is a story I teach each year. It brings forth an excellent discussion of reputation versus true character. It has a wealth of vocabulary and ideas for developing sentences, paragraphs, and even essays in the first several weeks of school depending on your grade level. You could have students create mini-board games using the vocabulary and other concepts from the novel. A homework assignment may be to play individually or with a partner at home as a review; students can also play the games in class. Again, they have learned the same concepts they would have if they were writing from a textbook, but this approach is so much more authentic. So they will be more inclined to do the work.

Your school or district may dictate exactly which picture books, novels, or other selections can be used in the classroom. And that is okay. It is the development of structured activities and lessons based on the selected literature that helps students make the needed connections.

So when *do* we use the textbooks? After all, the school board has mandated them; tax monies, PTO monies or your personal monies have paid for them. Why not use them? Do not get me wrong: I am not advocating that we throw out all the textbooks in our schools and start all over with something else. What I am saying is we have to make the lessons connect. We have to make what we are saying count. Often, the stories, activities, and examples in textbooks are not as authentic as the everyday experiences our children have. The textbook information is often not as current as what is in the latest online blog, local newspaper, or newest magazine article.

Therefore, we use our TCF standards of developing the students' values from within as our first goal. We connect our lessons by using activities we have created or borrowed from other teachers, using newspapers, television, reliable Internet sources, or innovative techniques we have picked up from our professional learning communities and professional literature. This approach is sure to draw and keep the students' attention.

Then, when we are ready to supplement, we should pull out the textbooks. This may be two or three times a week or two or three times in a grading period, depending on your subject area and the grade level you teach.

I make this point because of something I remember from a university student who we will call Kalen. She visited my school as a practicum student in the fall semester of one particular school year. While talking with Kalen, I asked what she thought made her want to learn, especially in a subject that she might perceive as her least favorite or most difficult. I told her that she could speak regarding her recent university courses, high school or any other level of schooling. She replied that it really did not matter. She simply said, "Make it fun." I asked her what that meant, and this was her response:

> Okay, one time I was in this class where we were studying Greece. The teacher read to us from the textbook and had us take some notes. But then after that, we just acted like we were from that country. We ate Greek food that we cooked, made projects that told us about the land and its people, and even memorized a poem from Greece. Then, we had to rewrite the poem in English. The group that had the best rewrite got a prize. So, you know, even though I didn't really like history, that's been my most fun class that I can remember. It was fun, you know. So that's what you should do.

What is that old saying—from the mouth of babes?

I know this concept may seem somewhat radical because we are usually encouraged to do just the opposite. Yet, we wonder why students come in upset, not wanting to learn, losing their textbooks (or pretending as such), and antagonistic toward the routines we have set. If we can just remember that it is all in the planning, it will become easier and easier as each day passes. We start on day one and continue with our efforts *consistently* through the rest of the year. We already know how to set up our day so students are ready to enter appropriately, work immediately, and expect something great when they walk into our rooms.

Now, all we have to do is keep their attention for the remaining grading periods. It sounds like a long time, but it goes quickly when you have your planning in place, connect the learning to real life experiences for students, and remember to be consistent. Do not forget it! One of my college professors used to remind us there is no such thing as being consistent most of the time. You either are or you are not. Those of us who are consistent set ourselves and our students up for a school year that will yield success. On the other hand, those who are occasionally consistent will see success elude them.

So our TCF code is in place, we are reviewing as we need to, students are engaged in the learning process; now what? Let us find out.

Table 6.1

Examples of Incorporating Character Education into Academic Themes

> Math: Multiply your successes!
>
> Science: Innovation at its best
>
> Social Studies: Good citizens make their mark!
>
> Reading: Be an original- no cheap copies here!
>
> Technology: Respect and responsibility—your computer's best friends
>
> Physical Ed.: Step into action; help others!
>
> Music: Delight your world one note at a time.

*These themes can be statements like we have listed here. Or, they can be singly worded thematic ideas. Keep the same overall theme for the entire year, or feel free to change the theme to go along with a subset of skills you are covering in a given time frame.

*Remember, the better you are able to relate ideas to both the character development and academic focus you have, the more the students will accept these ideas.

Table 6.2

Noun (or Verb) Web

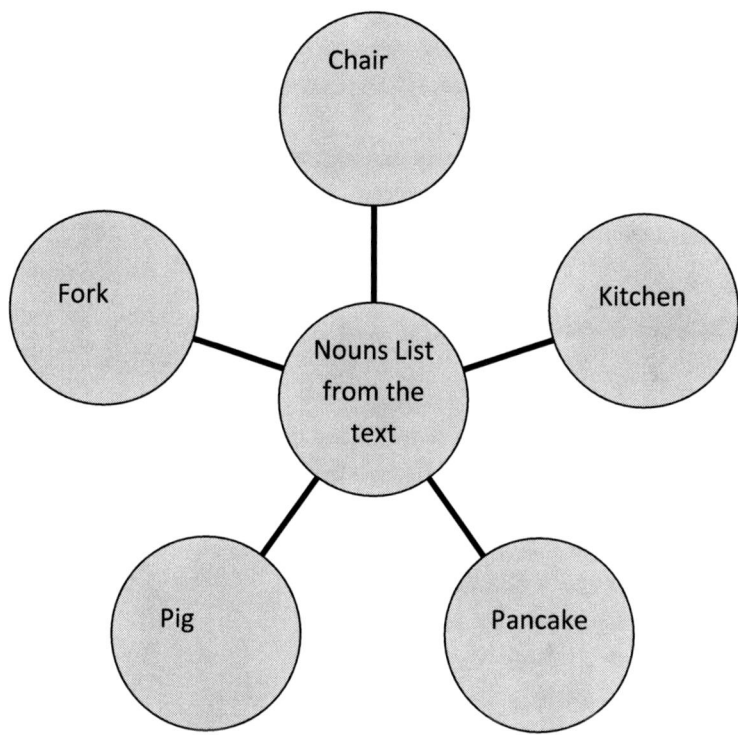

Created sentences:

1. Our new pig is greedy.
2. He eats at the table with a fork.
3. My pig's favorite food is pancakes.

*Note you could make the web as extensive or basic as needed, depending on the reading levels of your students. Just choose a different book.

*This can be modified and used with novels in the middle grades. Pull out the character traits, adverbs, ideas, etc., that a novel lends itself to as based on the standards or skills you are addressing.

Table 6.3

*Be sure to check for grade appropriateness before selecting the book to read aloud to your class. This is not a full bibliography. Rather, this list is a guide with which you can begin; you can find many more ideas online, at your public library in the children's section, or within your school districts' standards booklets.
*Some you can read aloud in one setting, others you can use over a week or longer to support a thematic focus, and some will be better for short excerpts in order to create student interest.

Read-Aloud Book List

- *I Like Me,* by Nancy Carlson
- *Madeline,* by Ludwig Bemelmans
- *Chicka Chicka Boom Boom,* by Bill Martin Jr. and John Archambault
- *Mrs. Piggle-Wiggle,* by Betty Macdonald
- *Stone Soup,* by Marcia Brown
- *The Giving Tree,* by Shel Silverstein
- *Rainbow Fish,* by Marcus Pfister
- *The Very Hungry Caterpillar,* by Eric Carle
- *Where the Wild Things Are,* by Maurice Sendak
- *Rough-Faced Girl,* by Rafe Martin
- *No David* (the entire series), by David Shannon
- *Junie B. Jones* (the series), by Barbara Park
- *Miss Rumphius,* by Barbara Cooney
- *Raising Dragons,* by Jerdine Nolen
- *Sylvester and the Magic Pebble,* by William Steig
- *A Chair for My Mother,* by Vera Williams
- *A New Coat for Anna,* by Harriet Ziefert
- *A Tree Is a Plant,* by Clyde Bulla
- *Adventure Stories that Will Thrill You,* by Reading Rainbow
- *Amelia Bedelia,* by Peggy Parish
- *Cloudy with a Chance of Meatballs,* by Judi Barrett
- *Horrible Harry* (the series), by Suzy Kline
- *Author's Mystery Envelope,* by Marc Brown

- *Caps for Sale*, by Esphyr Slobodkina
- *Bringing the Rain to Kapiti Plain*, by Verna Aardena
- *Tacky the Penguin*, by Helen Lester
- *The Velveteen Rabbit*, by Margery Williams
- *Because of Winn-Dixie*, by Kate Dicamillo
- *Bud, Not Buddy*, by Christopher Paul Curtis
- *Crispin*, by Avi
- *Every Girl Tells a Story*, by Carolyn Jones
- *The Giver*, by Lois Lowry
- *Stone Fox*, by John Reynolds Gardiner
- *Holes*, by Louis Sachar
- *My Side of the Mountain*, by Jean Craighead George
- *Roll of Thunder, Hear My Cry*, by Mildred Taylor
- *Tuck Everlasting*, by Nathalie Babbit
- *House of Dies Drear*, by Virginia Hamilton
- *Stargirl*, by Jerry Spinelli
- *Hoot*, by Carl Hiaasen

Chapter 7: Plan with Other Teachers as Often as You Can

MY AREAS OF EMPHASIS in teaching have been elementary and middle school. However, let us remember that any classroom established based on the TCF model will succeed no matter what grade level or subjects you teach.

So let us transition from our discussion of working with students for a moment and get down to the business of figuring out an effective way to work with other adults. We have talked about how to do things within your personal classroom, but what about everyone else around you? What about Mr. or Mrs. X, who has not read this book? And what about Mr. Y at the end of the hall, who would not participate in any type of professional development even if he were made to do so?

How do these teachers learn about the importance of engaging students, building character, and creating a class community in order to promote success? Well, it is your job to teach them. "My job!" you say. Yes, that is right! See, the biggest problem in education today is the same thing that is wrong with many other professions—the "me-my-I" syndrome. It is this feeling that what *I* have to say is right, what *I* do is great, and everything *I* touch is perfection because *I* say so. Now, that may be true for some people, so we will give those people the benefit of the doubt. Only what good is all that knowledge if you never share it with anyone else? It is no good. This is why sharing ideas, concerns, lessons, and activities among teammates remains critical in developing classrooms that affect our students in a positive way.

Sounds easy enough, right? So why do some teaching teams work well while others do not? Why do students seem to like Mrs. X and hate going to Mr. Y's class even though they are on the same team, teach the same grade, and there is nothing wrong with either teacher? More often than not, it is because the teachers are not on the same page. True enough, everyone has his or her own ideas about how things should go in his or her classroom, but there comes a point where you do have to get on the same page as far as what you expect of students in order to get similar results.

It puzzles me when teachers on teams I have worked with or teachers in my building who have heard how well things are going in my classes ask me how I do it. They ask in disbelief, "How in the world can you get those kids to do what you tell them to do?" I think to myself and often say aloud, "How do I do what?" Most inquiries center on how I get the types of students I have at each end of the behavior and academic spectrums to learn as much as I do in the way I do. The expectation is that because we work with difficult and often at-risk students, it is supposed to take some magic potion to get them to achieve anything significant.

I tell them I do not do anything (at least not anything magical). I set my expectations high, plan regularly, engage students in TCF learning from day one, and do not settle for anything less than excellence. I always invite my fellow teachers to come into my room and see how learning takes place. I also visit classrooms of teachers who use similar practices in their classrooms. I trust that each of us is able to see everything from the setup of the room to how the lesson is carried out; everything is connected.

Also, I visit other teachers' classrooms to see what innovative things they are doing to engage students in the learning process.
By inviting teachers to see what you are doing and plan with you, you are letting them see all of you are in it together. Too many times, our meetings with each other are only once week or once a month at a scheduled faculty meeting where we do not get to actually plan according to grade level or subject area. Or we have in-service days scheduled into our calendars, where a bunch of educational gurus come in and tell us how we are all doing it wrong and how to do it better. At some schools, we may even have a tradition of getting together socially for a meal before going away for the holiday or the end of school or something like that.

However, we must consider the necessity of forming more learning-focused meetings to seriously engage with one another. When we sit down on a more regular basis, we give ourselves an opportunity to observe several things.

- First, since many of us share students, we get to see which ones have consistent problems or successes in specific areas.
- Second, we get to discuss what works for us in regard to classroom management and other areas like getting homework turned in by most or all students.
- Next, we have a chance to share our own challenges within the classroom, whether it is with the curriculum, developing engaging activities, time management, parent contacts, etc.
- We also have a chance to talk with one another about any personal issues we deem necessary. We might need a chance to vent, share something positive, or just converse with adults for a moment after being with children all day.

The point is that when we are in open communication with those we teach with on a regular basis, we set ourselves up for success as a team. Do not be afraid to plan with your teammates. It does not mean you have to agree on every issue. Instead, it may often mean the need to agree to disagree with what others are saying. The point is you are in regular conversation about the students you serve.

This cuts down on students trying to pit teachers against one another. They know that what is expected by one teacher is going to be expected by the one across the hall and even the one downstairs on the other end of the building. This helps not only with establishing a positive classroom community but also a positive climate within your building, which leads to an overall positive school culture.

Here are some dos and don'ts to remember when setting up your team meetings.

- Do set a specific agenda.
- Do set a specific time.
- Do select a role for each team member to play, such as timekeeper, recorder, speaker, or materials manager, so everyone feels relevant.
- Do end at a comfortable time and put uncovered agenda items on the next meeting's agenda.
- Do remain positive, even when you do not agree.
- Do practice active listening.

- Do not come late to meetings!
- Do not get in the habit of settling for an email or newsletter rather than meeting face to face.
- Do not be negative.
- Do not miss meetings without a legitimate excuse. If you miss, do not forget to retrieve information you missed.
- Do not be the weakest link; if you are, seek assistance from your team members in order to become a better team player!

Some time frames that work for positive team planning are suggested below:

- Once a week in the mornings if you have a late school start time
- Once a week in the afternoons if you have an early school start time
- Biweekly at a set day according to subject area
- Biweekly according to grade level
- Biweekly according to special interests
- Biweekly to monthly as committees
- As deemed necessary by administrators in faculty meetings as an entire faculty
- Monthly in a social setting as team members, which will often lead to building solid professional relationships among those with which you work
- In scheduled conferences with parents
- In scheduled IEP or support team meetings with other teachers or parents

Again, the key with TCF teaming is the same as with our students—*consistency!* Remember when we meet, we must act professionally with one another. So many times, we do not model what we want students to say or do, but we wonder why they come into the classrooms argumentative, using inappropriate language, or nonchalant. Students are often mimicking what they see in us. We have to make our efforts in teaming just that—a team effort. It is the most effective way to be sure students develop the same behaviors. Start planning with your team *today*!

Chapter 8: TCF for the Teacher- Make Use of Professional Development Opportunities Early and Often

ONE OF THE PROBLEMS that plagues both new and seasoned teachers is the assumption that once we have adopted one method of doing something we have to keep doing things that way. On the contrary, teaching methods and styles need to be modified when necessary.

The students we encounter bring with them varying needs and abilities day to day and in some cases hour to hour. So, having the capability to deal effectively with such needs is a must. We cannot afford to become bored with what we are doing or seem boring to the students we serve.

This is why professional development is so important. It may seem unrelated to the TCF approach to teaching, but it is very much connected!

In many cases, school districts provide websites or local portals with information about professional development opportunities for teachers. Then, workshop sessions and seminars are divided into categories so teachers can get the most specific assistance possible according to their classroom needs.

For example, you may find something under the category of classroom management. Looking further, that could then be divided into segments having to do with organizing the physical space of the room, dealing with discipline, setting up your grade book or even varying your lesson presentations. Unfortunately, because of the size of many school districts, a professional development coordinator may not always be available to meet or talk directly with each teacher in reference to his or her specific needs. Therefore, it becomes a task that is left up to you. You must look at what is going on in your classroom in regards to the development of the TCF approach to teaching and see where you fit into this model. Before you can take what you have set up and carry it throughout the rest of the school year effectively, you must be willing to do what it takes to polish your skills as a teacher early on in the school year. Just as our students will not find real life connections in textbooks alone, neither will we find all the answers we need in our teachers' manuals. Team planning, which was discussed in the previous chapter, is just the beginning of this process of ensuring that our students receive access to the best we have to offer.

So, let us discuss critical types of professional development you should participate in as an individual.

#1 Classroom/Behavior Management

WHETHER IT IS A workshop session you attend, a book you read or an observation you make of another seasoned teacher is not the key here. What matters most is you choose one of these ways to make an ongoing assessment of your teaching and how you have or have not connected with your students early in the school year.

Many teachers make the mistake of thinking classroom management is just looking at the physical space in the classroom and how it is used. What teachers often forget is that once the physical space is set up effectively, we must continue to look at how the students respond to what is going on in this physical space. Are children sitting in rows, table teams, pairs? Are they actively engaging with one another at key points in your lessons? Or are they 'checking out' of the process? Have they become bored or disinterested in the activities and information you are presenting?

When students begin checking out of the learning process in your classroom, (and at times all students will) it is time to change the approach.

The best way to do this is to use your professional leave time to visit other teachers' classrooms who exhibit good classroom management skills. I talked a little about this in the last chapter focusing specifically on the teachers you work with on your team or in your grade level. However, it does not stop there. See what teachers are doing in other grade levels and even at other schools. Do not be afraid to see what others are doing and note that it may also work in your classroom. Take notes in detail. Look at the lesson subject the teacher is presenting. Observe the students particularly detailing the behaviors of those the teacher identifies as having behavioral and/or academic challenges. If teachers you observe have a handle on these children, you may be able to use what they are doing in your own classroom. It is often something as simple as what we are discussing in this book.

These teachers are probably using the TCF approach to learning and do not even realize it. It will be obvious because you will see all children engaged in the learning process. You will see the teacher using different methods throughout the lesson to get the point of the lesson across to the students. Also, you will notice an overall environment where textbooks and worksheets are used much less than hands on activities and discussions that draw students into the lesson objectives and goals that are being presented.

When observing other teachers' classrooms, it is important to visit the entire day or at the same time for a lesson series over the course of several days. This way you are able to look for patterns in the teachers' behaviors, students' behaviors and in methods used to get the lesson across to students. This is just as important in your own classroom. When you look at what begins working for you, you must look at the data you are gathering over time. One mistake we make when we try the TCF approach to creating lessons is changing something too soon.

For example, one of the most engaging ways to connect with students is by using games in lessons. However, the first time you introduce a game in connection with a lesson there may be a few who are so excited about something different that they do not display what they have learned by way of the TCF approach as they normally would. This becomes an opportunity for us to teach a mini lesson on how game playing should look in our classrooms. We cannot assume that because we give the directions for the game students will comply automatically. We must teach our students what we expect to see. Some teachers will see the undesirable behavior during the game playing scenario and stop using games in the classroom altogether. They go back to reading page whatever in the textbook and assigning often meaningless repetitive work for students to complete.

The difference in you and 'them' is because you know what works effectively with students, you will see what is working in other classrooms, model it for your students, and if a new method does not work exactly as you planned it the first time, you will tweak it and try again the next day. Any good research results will show that the researchers have looked at what has worked over time rather than discontinuing something that has presented difficulty in one setting.

I suggest using your time to visit other classrooms at least three times in a school year. This can be done midway through the first grading period while you are still planning and modifying what works for your students. It should be done at the beginning of the second semester when you have students who have moved away over the winter break and those who have moved into your class from other schools. This is important because it will also be the time of year when you are reviewing the TCF code and elements you have been using thus far in the school year with your students. Because the demographics of your classroom may change slightly with the addition of new students, this is an important time to look at what other teachers are doing that seems to be working as far as assisting new students with becoming part of your classroom community. Again, if you have been doing this all along, it will be easy. The end of the school year is also a good time to observe other teachers to see what types of skills and lessons they are preparing students to practice with over the summer months.

#2 Effective Use of Technology

ANOTHER GOOD AREA OF professional development all teachers need to explore is that of learning to use technology effectively in the classroom. There are numerous types of technology that can be used in the classroom at any grade level. However, when used ineffectively, it can destroy your TCF guidelines and progress you are making with your students.

When seeking out professional development opportunities in this area, teachers should look for sessions offered by the school district, local universities or even by way of webinars online right there in your classroom.

Most districts providing technology workshops start at the basic level by offering keyboarding classes, 'how to' sessions for Microsoft Office programs, and/or 'how to' sessions for using the Internet. If you are a teacher who has not used technology much in your personal time and who uses it even less in the classroom, this type of professional development is a nice starting point. By learning the basics of using the computer, you are better able to assist your students with classroom projects that include using the Internet for research. You are also able to help them complete projects or shorter assignments that require information be typed.

While it is perfectly fine to assign computer based assignments and projects outside the classroom, it is critical that technology based assignments be offered in the classroom setting as well. This is critical to making the TCF learning model work with students throughout the entire school year. One of the key parts to TCF, you will remember, is offering skills based teaching with something other than the textbook on a regular basis. With students being so technologically savvy, it is important that you show at least a basic knowledge of how to incorporate technology into your classroom regularly.

Another type of technology workshop that benefits teachers who use TCF with their students is one that focuses on showing teachers how to use videos, movies and digital books in the classroom. This is important because educational research has shown for many years that when we bombard students with digital images, they shut down almost immediately. Children do not benefit from watching an entire movie, viewing a lengthy video, or being shown an informative piece that is many minutes or hours long in one setting. Rather, when sharing information with students in a digital format, we should use short segments that are rich with the skills we want to address and are to the point. I generally use segments of information on a DVD, cd or Internet program that are eight minutes or less.

This holds the students' attention, prepares us for discussion of the topic, and sets them up for success later in the lesson when they are asked to work independently or in groups. Professional development in the area of technology is crucial not only because it is an effective way of sharing information and holding the interest of the students but because technology is so ever changing. Students have access to so many different technological devices that we have to keep up with what draws their interests in order to keep them focused on what they must learn academically in order to continue operating in this technological society successfully.

In the last pages of this chapter, you will notice I have provided worksheet style questions for you to print and reuse on your own as needed. These will be helpful anytime you are evaluating what types of classroom management or technology based professional development opportunities you need at a given time.

Worksheet #1

Professional Development: Classroom/Behavior Management

1. How are the students' desks set up in my room?
2. Is this set up useful when conducting activities with my students in small groups? during whole group lessons?
3. Are students with behavioral challenges participating effectively in activities?
4. Are students with academic challenges able to participate with others in their groups effectively?
5. Are students actively engaged in TCF learning? How do I know?
6. How often am I incorporating textbooks into lessons and discussions?
7. What other types of texts am I introducing into my lessons?
8. How many worksheets have I used with my students this week?
9. How many hands-on activities have my students participated in this week? month? grading period?
10. Based on my answers to the previous questions, what type of classroom or behavior management professional development do I need at this time?

Worksheet #2

Professional Development: Technology Use

1. How often do I use technology in my classroom at this time?
2. What does 'using technology' currently look like when I do use it with my students?
3. If I am using technology very little or not at all, what is the underlying reason?
4. Looking at the skills and subject areas I teach, what types of technology would benefit my students?
5. Do I know how to use abbreviated video segments with my students? How would the use of video segments benefit my students?
6. What is a webinar? What type of webinars would benefit me as a (enter your subject area name) teacher?
7. How do I currently use the Internet with my students? Is this benefiting them, or are there some modifications I need to make in this area?
8. Do I use projector based technology to read digital texts to/with my students? If not, why not?
9. Based on my answers to the previous questions, what type of technology based professional development do I need at this time?

Chapter 9: More TCF for the Teacher- Allowing Student Evaluations as another Type of Professional Development

SAY WHAT?

Yes- We must allow our students to evaluate us as teachers on a regular basis. I had to learn this the hard way.

As teachers, we are accustomed to having school administrators, parents and even visitors from school districts come in our classrooms and evaluate us in some way or another. However, when someone suggests we let the students participate in this process, we get nervous. Do we not? Yes. We say we are too busy, our lesson plans are too full; we know what the students will say. So what is the point?

The point is if we are going to develop an environment that truly fosters the spirit of community, we must include ourselves in that equation. So part of our ongoing professional development that helps our TCF approach to teaching continue effectively is allowing students to share with us what they feel works and does not work for them in our classrooms.

A Personal Story

MY FIRST FIVE OR so years of teaching were astoundingly difficult. Yet, I managed to remain positive and engage my students regularly refusing to give in to the challenges before me. I read them chapter books, introduced video clips to support skills taught, assigned projects and debates, cooked, conducted skits and even put on a play highlighting every child in the grade level one particular year.

For reasons I could not grasp at the time, all of this was not enough for my students. They obeyed me, but they also hated me. Year after year, the majority of my students did just what I assigned. Most of the homework assignments were completed in a timely manner. Most of the projects were completed and returned on schedule even if they were not up to par. Students participated in group activities in class if I asked them to. And so on it continued.

So what was the problem, and what helped me to identify it? Well, it is one of those things you find out from observing other teachers like we discussed in the last chapter.

One of my fellow teachers told me I was developing a reputation of being possibly the meanest teacher in the building. The kids all knew "Mrs. Tolbert [didn't] take no stuff." That is why they obeyed. It did not mean they had to like me in the face of that observation. So although they were somewhat participatory in class, this explained why some often seemed disconnected. The children still were not grasping overall concepts at the level I was seeking year after year.

I asked my teacher friend if she had any suggestions. She shared with me what she had done for years in each of her classes. "Let them evaluate you," she said. My fellow colleague and friend proceeded to explain what types of questions she posed to her students on a regular basis. She talked about having them note if what they were learning was fun. She shared that I should ask them what else they would like to learn. She suggested I also add questions about my teaching style or habits. Was there something I could be doing differently that they did not like? Or was there something I should add into our days that would appeal to them?

I pondered over this idea for a couple of weeks and finally decided to create an evaluation students could use to evaluate me. The results were jarring. Though I had been teaching middle school for several years at this point, I had no idea the students were so in tune to what should be going on in our classroom versus what was not. I remember sitting with my head in my hands and crying for several minutes upon reading the results of the first wave of evaluations. At that time, our school operated on an hour to hour class rotation schedule. So, for me, that meant a total of six evaluations that day. As you can imagine, by the end of the day I experienced six sets of evaluations that left me in tears.

Why? It was because I was so focused on trying to get my students to do what I wanted them to do that I forget to put myself in the TCF equation. You will remember a big part of *Teaching Character First* is making sure students know what respect looks like in your classroom. Well, this means remembering that not only are they watching and engaging with one another, but they are also observing us as the classroom facilitator.

In my case, students overwhelmingly noted that they enjoyed my class because it was fun. However, what I found disturbing was the landslide observation that I was "mean" because I "yelled all the time." The students saw this as "unfair" and wanted no part of it. As effective teachers should always do, I immediately began running through lessons, thematic units, talking with fellow teachers and close friends. "Do I yell?" "Am I mean?" These were just a couple of the questions I asked over and over again. These results were no different from what the children offered.

This was one of the main points in my teaching career which led to the development of the TCF approach to teaching and learning. I began recording my teaching sessions and playing them back at the end of the day. I needed to hear what they were hearing. I took my colleague's advice in that I also began letting the students conduct these evaluations at the end of each grading period. What I found was that I was yelling out key points to the lessons. I would raise my voice over students who were being disruptive because that is what I thought I had to do to get everyone else's attention. What the students were hearing was a mean young woman who spent all her time yelling "at" them. So, whenever I observed other teachers' classrooms, I made sure to notice what types of things they were doing to keep students engaged other than raising their voices. When students were off task, what did these teachers do to regain class structure?

What I noticed was that teachers who were engaging students in a more effective way were not raising their voices. These teachers were not forcing students to do anything. They were using TCF in a way that included them. These teachers were showing students how to act responsibly in class and how to respect one another by not only engaging them in lessons that were richer than a worksheet or textbook activity. They were modeling the behavior they wanted to see from the children.

So, I began adopting these principles myself. Each time I made an audiotape of my voice and listened to it I noticed changes. The year I started this process, I began to see that when students evaluated my behavior along with what was going on academically in class, they noticed the changes. Many even thanked me for speaking more softly, for ignoring student behaviors that were mildly inappropriate, and for trying to make learning fun everyday. Now, I do not have to cringe when I ask my students to evaluate me. No matter what grade level I am teaching, I am pleased with the results of the evaluations. Rarely do students have anything to say about something they see as objectionable or unpleasant. Often they go on and on about how much fun they are having, what they enjoy learning, and what they want to incorporate in the next grading period. That lets me know I am doing many things right.

How This Helps You Now

As you think about the challenges you face in your classroom, remember not to make yourself one of those challenges. Your students should be able to readily tell that you are dedicated to helping them learn in a safe and nurturing environment. They need to know you care enough to make sure you are living up to the same high expectations you have of them.

By making student evaluations part of your professional development schedule during the school year, you are able to hone in on what effect you are having on the students. You learn whether several of your students are already familiar with a concept. This helps ensure you do not waste time focusing on something they already know. It can also give you clues about how you may partner some students with others to review concepts that many understand but some do not. Ultimately, it will give you a clear picture of what the students see and hear as well as how they interpret it when you teach a lesson.

In the last pages of this chapter, take a look at the evaluation worksheets created for you. Remember to allow students to leave their names off of evaluations so they feel comfortable to answer openly. You can use these sheets as a guide according to your grade level. Print and reuse them anytime students evaluate you. Or, use them as a guide to creating your own. Either way, we must remember that high-quality teaching is only as excellent as our students perceive it. If they do not see us using the TCF concepts in all we do, our students will not either.

Worksheet #1

Elementary School Student Evaluation Questions

1. What did you do today that was fun?

2. What was not fun about your day?

3. What are you learning that is easy for you?

4. What are you learning that is hard?

5. Draw a picture of what you like about school.

6. Draw a picture of what you would like to learn tomorrow.

*Remember, children who are younger often interpret school as being fun or enjoyable when teachers engage them effectively. They often interpret school as not fun when teachers exhibit behaviors that are "unkind" and disengaging. This is the primary reason for the wording of the first two questions.

Worksheet #2

Middle School Student Evaluation Questions

1. During this grading period, what did you find most interesting?

2. During this grading period, what did you find least interesting?

3. What skills or concepts did you fully understand or already know at the beginning of this unit of study?

4. What skills or concepts do you still struggle with and wish the teacher would focus more on over the next several weeks?

5. What did the teacher do effectively this grading period to make learning worthwhile?

6. What can he or she do differently in the future to make learning more worthwhile?

Worksheet #3

High School Student Evaluation Questions

1. What skills or concepts did you fully understand or already know at the beginning of this unit of study?

2. What skills or concepts do you still struggle with and wish your teacher would focus more on over the next several weeks?

3. What did the teacher do effectively this grading period to make learning worthwhile?

4. What can he or she do differently in the future to make learning more worthwhile?

5. No matter your current grade, in terms of graduation, what is the most helpful thing you are learning in this class that will propel you into your next academic setting?

6. What real world connections can you draw from the information you are being presented with in this class?

7. If you could choose to take another class from this teacher in the future, would you? Why or why not?

Chapter 10: More on Management—How to Reach the Unreachable: Dare to Think Outside the Box

"ALL RIGHT," YOU SAY. "I have done everything you suggested in the TCF approach. I built the class routine, I have a theme each six weeks with activities to match, and I meet with my team regularly. I am ready to incorporate my textbooks now and teach the skills my district expects of me. Yet, I have two or three kids that are little holy terrors every class period. They destroy my whole class routine and climate on a weekly, almost daily, basis. I am at my wit's end! Where do I go from here?"

Actually, it is not as bad or as hard as you think. Really! You have reached the next step in planning a successful school year with the TCF model. That is, you have to actually reach the seemingly unreachable child!

Now, I know some people would argue all day long that you cannot save everyone who walks through the door, but how will we ever really know if we do not try? That does not mean try for a day or two and quit because the child has a wall up that cannot be permeated. Rather, it is all about being *consistent!*

Those two or three that seem unreachable have to know like the others that you care. Many times, we may be the only source of caring in these children's lives. So we have to make them know how much we care each and every day. Part of teaching character first is beginning with examining your own attitude and behavior you exhibit toward the children. If you do not care, have no worries. The children will know, and there will not be a bit of a difference you can make in their lives, their educations, or their treatment of you. Teachers who do not care about children should not be teachers.

See, for me, it is not some magic formula that makes it work in any of my classrooms. It takes lots of tolerance, love, compassion, and patience to get there. The key is that I never give up on my students. I have the children using the TCF approach because I care; they know it, and we reach our goals as a result.

Therefore, this chapter is devoted to two case studies of students I have taught who were thorns in my flesh for weeks and sometimes even months before we broke down their walls together. We will not discuss grade levels, so hopefully, you will see just how universal these problems and corrective approaches are. Just like the university student I spoke of before, the names will be changed to protect the identity of the children mentioned.

Let's begin:

1. Jeffry, elementary student: I taught this student about three years ago. I had only twenty-two students in my class that year, but Jeffry could have accounted for five others all by himself. You know the kind—always at your desk, always tattling on other students for looking at his paper or being too close to his desk, and so forth. Jeffry read at a level three years higher than his actual grade level and could have made As on everything he did. He qualified for gifted education classes but could not attend because of transportation conflicts. Jeffry was disliked by just about every student in the class, mainly because he annoyed them to no end. But he meant no harm; that was Jeffry being Jeffry. Everything he submitted, whether for a grade or for participation, had to have my stamp of approval. If I said it was nice, he smiled. If I said it needed work, he went back to his desk to work harder at it. However, one thing remained constant. Jeffry possessed the sloppiest handwriting of any child I have taught thus far who did not have some type of disability as an underlying factor. The handwriting was just sloppy for no apparent reason. And it took me a while to realize that the more I corrected him, the sloppier it got. Because things were not getting better with my occasional words of encouragement, I decided I would have to personalize my TCF approach with Jeffry.

I began digging into the respect and responsibility side of *his* life. I started looking at his work when he would bring it up to my desk and connecting it to real world happenings for him. For example, when we studied planets, I asked what planet he would like to travel to and why. I asked him what he would like to be in charge of on his planet if given the opportunity to choose. As he spoke, he began to reveal his true challenges. Jeffrey said, "Ms. T., I would make sure that all the little boys and girls there could have their own dad and that no one could ever come in and take them away. And if they did, I'd throw them off the planet and out into space. My planet, I think, would be Mars."

See, what was going on with Jeffry was not just that he was making below-average grades, doing below-average work, and aggravating the other children. It was not that he liked me so much that he longed to have a conversation about his work at my desk each day. The problem for Jeffry, I soon learned, was that his mom had just married a man who was not his father. This man was emotionally abusive to Jeffry and did not spend much time with him, and the family now had a new baby on the way. So Jeffry needed attention, and he would try to get it any way he could. Since I was his teacher, he picked me.

That is why the TCF approach to learning became so important for him. Jeffry would not automatically focus on skills alone. He had to be motivated extrinsically since he did not have it within the family structure. So I made Jeffrey my daily assistant. His jobs included changing the date, handing out materials for projects, and answering the class phone. Although all my other students also had jobs so as not to single Jeffry out, I made sure that his jobs were highly visible and made him feel a sense of self-worth that he may not otherwise have developed. Slowly but surely, Jeffry began to turn his sloppiest handwriting into minimally sloppy handwriting. And the sidebar conversations he always needed to have at my desk about what everyone except him in the class was doing wrong eventually stopped.

The point was Jeffry had to feel as though he belonged before he would open up to focusing on his skills work. He had to see not only was he respected by me but he was also expected to follow through with the responsibilities I presented to him. I am proud to say that Jeffry made it through the school year with B averages in all his subjects and a smile on his face to lead him into the next school year.

2. Andrea, middle school student: I taught Andrea in the second year of my teaching career. Let me tell you, I did *not* think both of us would make it through that year alive! You know the kind of years. Oh, and in case you are wondering, I was the one headed to an early grave! At twenty-three years old, I thought, *What on earth have I gotten myself into? This is not what I signed up for!*

Andrea's problem—everything. From the moment she entered my room, she decided that she hated me, my class, anything I was teaching, all the students, and life in general. I would greet the students as they entered, and she would sarcastically say to me, "Mum hum, hey, girl" (among other things). I could put the students in groups for an activity, and she would open a magazine and start reading and talking loudly about whatever it was that interested her. She filed her nails, combed her hair, yelled out, "This **** is boring. Ugh!" and so many other lovely things that run a class climate directly into the ground. Well, I immediately thought, *This girl is over the top. I have to get her out of this room. If not, she is going to ruin everything I have worked so hard to develop with my other students.*

My problem—the school administrators did not agree. The principals promptly let me know that they already knew "how she was," and there was nothing anyone could do about it. The other teacher on my team could not handle her, and so I would have to do the best I could with what I had. Well, "what I had" was a student who yelled obscenities in the middle of my lessons, called me names openly in front of other students, and refused to complete any amount of work assigned to her by me or anyone else in the school.

Initially, I thought I could quit and just try another path to a successful career. Instead, I decided to at least try some TCF planning with Andrea. Understand that I was well aware of the fact there was no way Andrea could remain in my actual classroom for the rest of the year. That would have been detrimental to the other students as well as to my emotional well-being as a new teacher. So I began some creative planning. I went directly to Andrea in class one day right outside my classroom and asked her how she would feel about being excused from my class for the rest of the year. Of course, Andrea was thrilled. She let me know rather quickly that she did not need my class or any other. Andrea was independent enough to deal with life on her own both in school and at home.

So I went to the librarian as well as my administrators. I asked the librarian how she would feel about me setting up an independent learning program with Andrea in the library. I agreed to do all the work, all the checking up, all the assessments, and the progress monitoring with Andrea. All the administrators had to do was support me; all the librarian had to do was provide the space. They each agreed it would be fine but strictly up to me to make it work.

Later that week, I met with Andrea and her mother, letting them know how slowly she was progressing overall and that she was on the verge of failing for the school year. At her age, she could not afford to fail again. However, Andrea was determined to drop out of school as soon as she turned eighteen anyhow. She shared that fact with me on as many occasions as possible. Andrea's mother told me she really did not care what Andrea did. She had eight other children at home she was raising on her own, and Andrea was the oldest. She could "sink or swim," as her mother put it. She did not really care.

Well, trying a bit of reverse psychology, I assured Andrea that since she was not old enough to drop out yet, I could make the rest of the school year a little less painful by allowing her an independent learning environment in which she could manage herself. It was the first of several TCF incentives I tried with her. Much to my surprise, Andrea agreed to do the independent learning program if I agreed to leave her alone the rest of the year. So we agreed to disagree, and the challenge was on.

Please understand that I am including this specific case study example for the purpose of showing you the TCF approach is not a walk in the park. It is something you must commit to or, like any other idea, it will not work.

I spent the next several days transferring lesson information from my desktop computer to a hard copy file for Andrea. I set up dates, grades to aim for, and an explanation of each assignment. In the packet for each grading period, I provided worksheets, suggested novels, connective texts within our textbook series, and projects she would complete and report aloud directly to me rather than in front of her peers.

I kid you not, in about three days or so, I heard nothing more from Andrea. I would peek into the library, and she would be reading, walking around researching the library area, or working hastily to complete some project. The librarian helped her when she asked, and when I came in and asked how it was going, what struck me the most was there was no yelling. There was no name-calling, no throwing pencils, no screaming that she hated me, just a student hard at work to reach whatever that week's goal was.

And this was how TCF worked for Andrea. See, for whatever reason, she was not able to work in the regular classroom setting. She did not qualify for any special programming, did not qualify for a discipline program for fragile students, and did not have any apparent learning disabilities or delays. The only thing wrong with Andrea was she was smothering. At home, she helped with the eight other children while her mother was at work. Sometimes, her mother did not get home until after 11:00 p.m. So Andrea had no room in her mind for someone else to give her even more responsibilities to complete in groups of other peers and so forth. She had no room in her mind for yet another adult telling her what to do. She needed some quiet time to be at peace with herself and truly figure out what it was she needed to be doing with her life.

Andrea passed that school year with Cs in my class. She passed her other classes as well. I was never quite sure what happened to her once she left our school. Then, it happened. I saw Andrea years later at a gas station just outside of one of our local venues one evening on my way back to my car coming from a Monday night football game. Though I did not recognize her at first, she made sure that did not last very long. The door was locked where apparently they had just closed the inside part of the gas station area for the night. I pulled on the door and was headed back to my car when I heard someone yell, "Ms. Tolbert, Ms. Tolbert. Hey!" I turned around, thinking, *Oh boy, I wonder who that is this late at night.* As I got closer, I realized it was one of my former students from many years ago. It did not take long for me to call her full name at once, too. I knew exactly who she was and was frankly quite surprised to see her doing anything positive. I asked Andrea what she had been up to and what she was doing with her newfound freedom from school.

She told me she had graduated the previous spring and was working her way through junior college. She wanted to be a nurse. I told her to keep up the good work and that she would go as far as she could ever imagine.

Andrea simply put her arms around me and said, "I could not have gotten this far without you. Thanks. And I'm sorry I was so hard on you."

With a smile, I said, "No. Thank you. Good luck!" And with that, we were both on our way.

Much like with Jeffry and Andrea, success for many students does not start and end with the textbook series or throwing skills and tests in front of our children's faces. It starts with a TCF model that includes responsibility and respect within one's character and then grows forth from that. See, engaging students from day one is not a novel concept. It is a necessity. Look at how involved children become in day-to-day hobbies. No children choose to play the violin or soccer because they hate doing it. Children select these hobbies because upon engaging in them continually, they find themselves. Children find what works for them.

Reaching students in the classroom setting is so very similar. We pull the strategies that work; focus on individual student learning modalities; add in our skills, textbooks, projects, etc.; and watch our students bloom. But without a focus that is as direct and as well planned as this, we are not only failing ourselves—we are failing our children.

So where do we go from here? How does all this end?

Turn the page and let us see.

Chapter 11: Putting It All Together

I KNOW ALL OF this sounds great, but much as it is with other prospective ideas we seek to implement in the classroom, we still wonder where the starting point should be. I would suggest that you make things as simple as possible.

TCF, *Teaching Character First*, is simple. Use the following checklist to start your school year and follow through for the rest of the year:

- Remember that the TCF teaching strategy takes dedication.
- Engage your students from day one as soon as they arrive. Greet them every day.
- Be prepared for the first five days with TCF implementation.
- Develop your TCF code with students and begin modeling.
- Teach skills based on the character traits you want to emphasize.
- Gear your lessons toward the multiple intelligences/varied learning modalities.
- Role-play situations involving respect and responsibility.
- Select your theme and prepare to reference it throughout the entire school year.
- Plan with your teammates often, deliberately, and positively.
- Be prepared for out of the box thinking and activities in order to reach the otherwise "unreachable."
- Keep parents informed at all times.
- Begin each day with your focus in mind, and then go for it!
- Add in your textbooks *as needed* in order to supplement what you are teaching.
- Remember, you can use rubrics, projects, discussion, paper/pencil, and so much more than just textbooks to get educational objectives across to your students.
- Remember, you will be behind some of your teammates if you start your school year by using the TCF approach.

However, that is fine, because later in the semester when they are still fighting behavior battles, you will have surpassed them greatly!

I hope that by sharing my ideas with you, it helps you in beginning a successful school year with your students. Keep in mind that the TCF concept is more of a guide than anything. It does not remove the use of a text in your classroom. On the contrary, a lot of what we introduce to students comes from some form of a written text. Remember, we cannot solely rely on those resources to reach our students. This is what the TCF model keeps at the forefront of our minds.

In recent years, something has happened to us as educators. We have forgotten what it is that we do best—*educate*! It does not matter if we are in the public sector or private, whether we work with pre-K through elementary, middle, or high school. We *can* still make a difference in the lives of our students if we try.

Do what you know works! You have skills lists, state and national standards, and more test prep books and assessments than you will ever need or use in many cases.

The only thing left for you to do is actually teach. Think out of the box with me for one school year. Commit to using TCF prior to anything else, and you will see that the sky is truly the limit for you and your students. You will automatically do it again the following year!

Stop being afraid that you will not hit every skill and every sub-skill your district throws your way. The bottom line is that if you will actively engage students from day one, their brains will follow because *they* will see to it that it happens. Then, skills are easier to manage and lives are easier to change.

I have given you the tools. I hope I have motivated you to believe in what you set out to do as the wonderful educator you know yourself to be.

So now it is your turn. Throw the textbooks aside today, and teach character first. Your students will thank you!

Resources

Block, Peter, *The Answer to How Is Yes: Acting on What Matters.* San Francisco: Berrett-Koehler, 2003.

Bolman, Lee, and Terrence Deal, *Leading with Soul: An Uncommon Journey of Spirit.* San Francisco: Jossey-Bass, 1996.

"Bush: NCLB not meant to punish schools, but to help them," *CNN*, April 12, 2007, http://www.districtadministration.com/newssummary.aspx?news=yes&postid=18883.

Covey, Stephen, *Principle Centered Leadership.* New York: Simon and Schuster, 1992.

Fuller, Howard and George Mitchell, "A Culture of Complaint," *Education Next* 3 (2006): http://media.hoover.org/documents.ednext20063_18.pdf.

Gladwell, Malcolm, *The Tipping Point: How Little Things Can Make a Big Difference.* New York: Back Bay Books, 2002.

Gurian, Michael, *Boys and Girls Learn Differently.* New York: John Wiley and Sons, 2001.

Heacox, Diane, *Differentiating Instruction in the Regular Classroom.* Minneapolis, MN: Free Spirit Publishing, 2002.

Hamel, Gary, *Leading the Revolution.* Cambridge, MA: Harvard Business School, 2002.

Marzano, Robert, *What Works in Schools: Translating Research into Action*. Alexandria, VA: Association for Supervision and Curriculum Development, 2003.

National Commission on Excellence in Education, *A Nation at Risk*, April 1983, http://www.2.ed.gov/pubs/NatAtRisk/index.html.

Stevenson, Harold, and James Stigler, *The Learning Gap: Why Our Schools Are Failing and What We Can Learn from Japanese and Chinese Education*. New York: Simon & Schuster, 1992.

CPSIA information can be obtained at www.ICGtesting.com
226350LV00001B/16/P